Punny, ha, ha

A book of original jokes by Stuart Skyte

Cartoons by Meg Barton

GW00392224

Introduction

After a career in "not-for-profit" public relations, I retired early and decided, among other things, to write.   "Punny, ha, ha" is my first book of jokes. No surprise that I'm sometimes called "a groan man". Some of my short plays have been put on in Oxford as part of events organised by Oxford Playwrights.

There are two people I would like to thank: my wife, Gillian, who has put up with my "jokes" for 45 years, and one of her oldest friends, Meg Barton, who has drawn the cartoons. Thank you, both.

Stuart Skyte
November 2023

You have to start somewhere….

Everyone these days is into genealogy. Even Goldilocks is trying to trace her forebears.

I was fed up with having a bad back so often that I went to see a witch doctor. He said I needed a spell in hospital.

My dentist said I should look after my teeth as they don't grow on trees. I said what about gum trees?

Did you hear about the monk who used to go to a nudist colony for his holidays but has got out of the habit?

I passed this man begging in the street. He asked me to help him as he had had both his feet amputated. I told him that, while I was sympathetic, I was lack-toes intolerant.

Did you hear about the English king who agreed with everything he was told? He was William the Concurrer.

And what about the man who attacked people's belly buttons? He was a navel destroyer.

My optician told me she was packing her job in to rear pigs. She had her eye on a stye.

What do chickens do when they want to get up early? They set their alarm cluck.

I was pleased to learn about the pet-friendly service offered by our local council. You can leave your car and your dog in a designated area while you go shopping in the centre of town. It's a "bark and ride" scheme.

Did you hear about the composer who was 99% French and 1% Australian? He was barely Oz.

Talking of France, when I was there recently, I ate an omelette every day. That was more than an oeuf.

Did you hear about the flower-sellers who fell in love? They put their tulips together.

How does a brass player keep his instrument clean and shiny? He uses a tuba toothpaste.

Did you hear about the vicar who grew a massive pumpkin? Gourd almighty.

What is the difference?

What is the difference between the alphabet and a women's public toilet? In the alphabet, P always comes before Q but, in a women's public toilet, Q is often before P.

What is the difference between spending two hours in a coffee shop and grieving? One is passing the morning and the other is mourning the passing.

What is the difference between a bird-watcher, a sex-mad vicar and a bad-tempered watch-maker? One is an ornithologist, one is a horny theologist and one is a thorny horologist.

What is the difference between a lover of Indian food and someone who crawls to his boss? One favours curry and the other curries favour.

Did you hear about?

Did you hear about the man in Athens who collects paper-clips and designs computer games? He's Zorba the Geek.

Did you hear about the man who hits people over the head with Weetabix? He's a cereal killer.

Did you hear about the heart surgeon who is scruffily dressed? He wears a tacky cardigan.

Did you hear about the man who has 50 pairs of swimming trunks? He's a Speedophile.

Did you hear about the pop-star who kept books in his toilet? Lou Reed.

Did you hear about the group of women musicians who play in their underwear? They're a bras band.

Did you hear about the cross-dressing cricketer? He never bowls without a slip.

Did you hear about the couple whose house was on the edge of the white cliffs of Dover? They had ferries at the bottom of their garden.

Did you hear about the low-paid vegetable peeler? He just about scrapes a living.

Did you hear about the elderly vegetarians? They were has-beans.

Did you hear about the Frenchman who sat on his baguette? He had a pain in his bum.

Did you hear about the gravediggers who went on strike? They took industrial inter-action.

Did you hear about the American Indian who drank 12 cups of Earl Grey? He had a lot of tea pees.

Did you hear about the nutcase who joined the army? He became a kernel.

Did you hear about the promiscuous RAF pilot? He's a flighty officer.

Agriculture, animals & birds

A farmer had a vineyard and a flock of sheep, so she opened a wine baa.

Did you hear about the cowhand who went part-time? She works every udder day.

Why did the cow stamp her foot? She was in a bad moooood.

Why didn't the landscape painter set up his easel at the pig farm? It was a porcine.

Why did the leopard hide behind a tree? He didn't want to be spotted.

What do you call a bird with asthma? A puffin.

Did you hear about the pair of herons who decided not to have babies? They had no egrets about the decision.

What do you call a small mad rodent with flowers in its hair? A hippy, potty mouse.

What do noisy pigeons wear? Coulottes.

What did the Nepalese sherpa say when he saw his cockerel sitting on an egg? Him-a-layer.

What do chickens do when they want to get up early? They set their alarm cluck.

I went into my local pet shop to buy a kitten. I was rather surprised by the sign up in the cat area which read: "Buy one, get one flea"

What do you do when your kitten can't focus and keeps falling asleep? Give the catatonic.

Why?

Why did the cricketer need an operation? He had one short square leg and one long leg.

Why did the spy need a handkerchief? He had a code in his nose.

Why did the paper-maker wake up in a sweat in the middle of the night? He was having a bad ream.

Why did the paper-maker grin from ear to ear? He'd made a heavenly quire.

Sex

Some people love nothing better than spending all day in the kitchen cooking. They must be pan-sexual.

Some people love nothing better than spending all day shopping. They must be buy-sexual.

My favourite holiday destination in the world is the Italian Lakes. I must be Comosexual.

Classical music

The composer Richard Wagner kept a herd of cows. One had a great sense of humour; Wagner would tell her a joke and she would low an' grin.

Which composers should you always take to the supermarket? Chopin Liszt.

Did you hear about the composer who always wore a turban? He was Haydn Sikh.

Did you hear about the composer who had a noisy dog? It would often bark.

Why was the tone-deaf singer locked out of his home? He couldn't find the right key.

What is a wind musician's favourite
sandwich?   Cheese and piccolo.

Why do brass-players never lose a game of
bridge? Because whatever card their
opponents play, they'll always trumpet.

What do you call someone who steals
music?   A cleftomaniac.

Did you hear about the musician who was
run over by a steam-roller? He was B flat.

What do you get if you cross a musical
instrument with a fish? A piano tuna.

Did you hear about the musician who
answered every question on University
Challenge? He was F sharp.

The composer Richard Strauss couldn't abide small rodents. He once flayed a mouse he found in his kitchen.

How do you contact a brass-player urgently? Euphonium.

What musical instrument does a cockney tramp play? The oboe.

What do you call a soprano in a submarine?
A deep-sea diva.

Fishermen's top-ten favourite tunas:

I could have included a lot more of these in the book but I didn't want to fillet with fish jokes. Tench is more than enough:

- O coley night
- On herring the first cuckoo in spring
- O cod our help in ages past
- The shark ascending
- I had a bream
- Somewhere over the rainbow trout
- Fool on the brill
- Heaven is a plaice on earth
- Mozart's flute & carp concerto
- Prawn to be wild

Bird-watchers' top-ten favourite dove songs

Again, the temptation was to include more than ten, but I didn't want to engender owls of frustration from the readers when they are desperate to tern the page.

- You'll never hawk alone
- Move over starling
- Grouse of the rising sun
- Teal meet again
- Silent kite
- Long-haired plover from Liverpool
- Gull of Kintyre
- Crow me the way to go home
- Wren I fall in love
- Rook through any window

Food & drink

Who says you can't eat your words? What about paperback raita?

My father was a baker, as was his father before him. I was a baker, born and bread. I knew my roll in life. I remember my father saying to me that I would knead to be a baker.

I parked our vintage car outside a French café. The waiter came out and said "I like your crock, monsieur."

Did you hear about the idiotic chef who was always making nasty comments? He was a rude barb fool.

Did you hear about the man who eats Australian shoes for his breakfast? He has scrambled Uggs on toast.

A little boy told his mother he wanted some small round green vegetables. She said: "Where's your manners? Say peas."

Did you hear about the woman who took a load of soft dried fruit to the bank? She wanted to open a currant account.

I spoke to the man who had just broken the world record for eating hot dogs. I asked him: How many did you eat, how did you eat them and what gave you the strength to do this? He said one word: 40-chewed.

I complained to the waiter in the coffee shop that I'd been waiting an hour to be served. He said it was better latte than never.

What do you call someone who loves Turkish bread? A pidephile.

Why did the fishmonger ignore the customer's complaint? Because his herring was bad.

Why did the tourist get lost in Dijon? He mustard taken the wrong turning.

Why was the greengrocer so sad? He was full of melon-cauli.

I'm starting a business selling eggs on line. Customers have to pick up their orders as I don't deliver. It's cluck and collect.

What did the fishmonger say to the greengrocer when he wanted to ask her out on a date? If you've got the thyme, I've got the plaice.

Did you hear about the cannibals who ate an academic for their dessert? The prof was in the pudding.

Why couldn't the Dutchman sell his cheese? Because it was madE back to front.

A police officer walked into a restaurant and said he wanted to book a table. The waiter objected and said the table had done nothing wrong.

Gardening

I asked the vicar his secret for growing perfect salad crops. He said it was very simple; lettuce pray.

Did you hear about the snooty gardener? He was a haughty culturalist.

Did you hear about the gardener who planted lots of grass-seed but wasn't optimistic about it growing? It was a for-lawn hope.

If there's one flower I hate, it's Anemone.

Where do you put flowers to make them last for months? In the Freesia.

When is a garden a waste of time? When there's no Fuchsia in it.

I read this book about a gang of crooks who went round stealing trees. It was a classic copse and robbers story.

What tree can you take on holiday? Acacia clothes.

What tree can you be related to? Cistus.

What tools do you need to dig up trees? Acer spades.

What did the tree say when it felt it was getting too big? Prunus.

How do you ensure ground-cover grows well? Poor Ajuga water on it each week.

What do you call?

What do you call a man who is always demanding money? Bill.

What do you call a cockney man who doesn't drink pints? Alf.

What do you call a woman who is always getting stoned? Olive.

What do you call a man who prays every day? Neil.

What do you call a mountain-climber with a guitar? A rock musician

What do you call a singing fish? A sea bass.

What do you call someone who does mindfulness exercises naked? Yoga Bare.

Christmas

Why was Father Christmas told off when he came down the chimney? Because he'd made a grate mess.

What's Father Christmas's favourite drink? Fanta Claus.

Why does Father Christmas never plan ahead? He only lives for the present.

Have you ever wondered who decides what Christmas decorations appear in the shops each year? I've discovered there's a small group of people responsible. They're a self-appointed holly-garchy.

Why was Father Christmas sad? Because
he'd got the sack.

...and finally

I like continuing education and learning new things, but I draw the line at art classes.

Our roof is leaking. It's problem attic.

Where's the best place to buy an engagement ring? On a jewel carriageway.

I was devastated when my washing dryer stand collapsed. It was the end of an airer.

Printed in Great Britain
by Amazon